MINISTRY
and the
MIRACULOUS

MINISTRY
and the
MIRACULOUS

A case study at
Fuller Theological Seminary

Edited by
LEWIS B. SMEDES
with a Foreword by
DAVID ALLAN HUBBARD

MINISTRY AND THE MIRACULOUS

Copyright © 1987 by Fuller Theological Seminary

Library of Congress Cataloging-in-Publication Data

Ministry and the miraculous.

    1. Spiritual healing.   2. Spiritual healing—
Study and teaching (Graduate)—California—Pasadena.
3. Miracles.   4. Miracles—Study and teaching
(Graduate)—California—Pasadena.   5. Fuller
Theological Seminary.   I. Smedes, Lewis B.
II. Fuller Theological Seminary.
BT732.5.M556   1987   231.7′3′071179493   87–2156
ISBN 0–8499–3075–8

Printed in the United States of America

7898FG987654321

Contents

MINISTRY
and the
MIRACULOUS

Foreword

- Does Christ heal today as he did on the pages of the Gospels?
- Does life in the Spirit always carry with it good health, physically and emotionally?
- Is medical care a last resort or the first line of defense for Christians?
- Has something gone wrong when godly people are chronically ill?
- How do we explain why God heals some persons and not others?
- Is an emphasis on miraculous healing more suited to mission contexts where medical resources are not readily available?

My childhood confronted me with these questions from the cradle. They were regular table talk in my home from high chair through high school. Prayer for sick people—whether family, church members, or outsiders—was as much a part of our household routine as Saturday cleaning, Tuesday night prayer meeting, or summer canning. Though we had two medical doctors who attended our church during my childhood, I could count on the fingers of one hand the times they visited our home for professional reasons. Prayer and some homespun remedies were the ways in which we coped in the twenty years between our move to Oakland, California, in 1932 and my father's sudden death of cardiac arrest in 1952.

Not that we were sheltered from the assaults of disease or accident. I had all the standard childhood ailments. My older brother, in his twenties, had mumps with serious complications. My foster sister died of tuberculosis as a newlywed. My mother was severely scarred in the explosion of a pressure cooker. My father spent months in bed after an initial heart attack in 1944. A bee sting sent an allergic reaction through my system that grievously impaired my breathing. Throughout these experiences we rejoiced in God's loving power when each family member was spared, and we accepted the goodness of God's will when our foster sister was taken.

What sharpened most acutely for me the questions about God's ways was my sister Laura's eye trouble. Eleven years older than I, she had been born with an ocular weakness that resulted in sharply crossed eyes when she was a toddler. Thick lenses were her constant companion and nagging irritation through her whole career in school. Valedictorian of her high school class, she had to leave the university in her freshman year because her eyes could not handle the heavy demands of reading. And all the while voluminous amounts of prayer were being offered on her behalf. Each visiting evangelist or Bible teacher presented fresh opportunity for her healing. Hands were laid on her; she was anointed with oil; Satan's power was rebuked and Jesus' name invoked. Her eyes, however, remained crossed.

Laura and I were very close. She was my main source of care, training, and support during my childhood days, when my parents were relentlessly occupied with their duties as co-pastors of our little church. I sensed her struggles of hope and disappointment, and her puzzlement and frustration became part of the curriculum in which I first wrestled with the whys of divine providence.

Simple answers pondered then and now by well-meaning but unthinking practitioners of divine healing I rejected out of hand. "Not enough faith" or "sin in your life" I intuitively recognized as formulae inappropriate and inadequate to explain my sister's experience. People in our circle whose lives seemed to me neither to glow with faith nor sparkle with righteousness were healed, and Laura was not. For me the trite explanations of why she was not healed bristled with problems. For one thing they were hard on her. Absence of faith or presence of sin as pat reasons for chronic illness or physical limitation only lay heavier loads on already over-burdened people. Blame bordering on rejection is no comfort to those whose sense of worth is already worn paper thin by the chafing cords of pain and inadequacy. But the One who suffers most in such circumstances is God. Setting fixed terms which decide whether he performs healing or not nudges us across the border that separates providence from magic and trespasses on God's right to be Lord. It preempts his authority to decide when and how to manifest his power. It makes our conformity to certain conditions rather than his sovereignty the ultimate ground of how he works. In the process, everyone loses. We find it hard to cling to God's love when healing does not take place, and God becomes servant of our needs and not Master of our destiny.

My parents' steadfast faith in God and wise application of biblical truth was also a major part of this boyhood curriculum, along with Laura's patient struggle with infirmity and her warm-hearted consistency in serving Christ. Theologically trained—Dad at Drew University, Mother at Biblical Seminary, New York—my parents skirted the pitfalls of simplistic explanations for the absence of healing even though they based large portions of their ministry on God's power and willingness to heal. Every Sunday morning service, every Tuesday and Friday evening Bible study included prayer for the sick, not to speak of the all-day prayer sessions which occupied most Tuesdays. And to anoint the sick my Father carried a vial of olive oil in his inner pocket alongside his fountain pen, the former just as essential to his daily rounds of pastoral ministry.

Their classical theological training was not so much altered as expanded, when, in 1923, they entered into a pentecostal experience and began personally to know the relevance of the dramatic spiritual gifts of 1 Corinthians 12 for the church. Their solid commitment to biblical authority and their broad knowledge of the biblical message in its many and diverse facets kept their charismatic activity in balance—and also helped them to support Laura in her particular plight. More by their attitudes than their declarations, they taught us that God was no less good when he did not heal than when he did, that his compassion sometimes showed itself in the working of miracles and other times in the withholding of miracles, that God's task was to decide what was best and ours was to accept that decision with love and faithfulness.

Years of missionary service in Puerto Rico set their cross-cultural stamp on my family. Many of our closest friends were missionaries, some of whom lived with us months at a time on furlough. Talk turned frequently to the dark powers that seemed obvious and persistent in non-Christian cultures. The gifts of the Spirit were treasured by these missionaries as the only adequate antidote to the demonic and the only available panacea for illness in places remote from medical help. What to my boyish mind seemed an extraordinary form of spiritual commitment—to depend daily on God for aid that others sought from pharmacist and physician—appeared to be a necessity in the distant settings where our friends labored. There the confrontations with evil were as unsubtle as a frontier showdown. It was missionary versus shaman in a conflict as bold as Elijah's with the Baal priests on the brow of Carmel.

At times life in our small congregation took on the character of that primal power-encounter. The father of my two closest friends had been an alcoholic since his teen years. No treatment of any kind had produced permanent relief until in despair he committed himself to the devout band of women ("prayer-warriors" we called them) who fasted and prayed each Tuesday for the needs of the church and the world. After a wrenching struggle, demons were cast out; he remained free of the clutches of alcohol for the rest of his life.

Subsequent years of ministry in higher education, radio, and the pastorate have only confirmed, refined, and expanded the insights gained from scores of conversations at our kitchen table and hundreds of experiences in the services of our church; regular dependence on the power of God (a lesson underlined dozens of times during the chronic bouts with ill-health endured by my wife, Ruth); firm belief that miracles did not cease when the Scriptures were completed; growing recognition that the God of miracles and the God of medicine were the same Person working in different ways, at different speeds, and for different purposes; increased awareness that divine goodness worked both through suffering patiently borne and through healing exuberantly received; and a yielding to God's will at all points, even in the loss of an eight-week-old son born with a cluster of congenital anomalies.

Further reflection added to the list of insights. Miracles do not occur evenly throughout the course of salvation history as recounted in Scripture, but they come in batches at times selected by God: the Exodus and wilderness wanderings, the crucial days of Elijah and Elisha when the purity of Israel's worship was at stake, the introduction of the kingdom in the life and ministry of Jesus, the expansion of the church in the stories of Acts. The theological conclusion to be drawn from the Bible's own use of the miraculous seems clear: the primary motive for divine miracle is not compassion but revelation. We can assume something like a consistent level of pain and suffering in the world this side of our human fall. The need for divine compassion is, then, a virtual constant. Yet the exercise of that compassion to heal is *sporadic in Scripture* and apparently in the centuries that have followed. Indeed, God's providence has shown itself at least as frequently in permitting the persecution of his people or subjecting them, along with others, to natural disasters—earthquake, fire, flood, plague, drought—as in miraculously restoring them to health. Whenever we deal with the ways of God, we are dealing with bright mysteries that leave us squint-eyed and blinking when we stare them full in the face.

As Christians whose primary ministry is scholarship, we bow before these mysteries, but we do not back away from them. Part of our service to the church is to study the complex, to sort out the intricate, to scrutinize the puzzling. It is our responsibility to face the tough questions put to us by the Scriptures, the churches, and the contemporary world. It has meant since our founding that we must hazard the risks necessary to break fresh ground in ministry and broach new ideas in scholarship. We have felt it our duty to put our biblical convictions into practice, even when the price is high, as well as brave the potential dangers of our mistakes and criticisms of those who may misunderstand. As part of the vanguard of God's educational enterprise, we have assumed these as guiding imperatives for our life as an academic institution under the Lordship of Jesus Christ.

For these reasons and because of my personal background, I welcomed the inauguration in 1982 of a course in the role of the miraculous in the growth of the church. The catalog listing was MC510 and the official title was the *Miraculous and Church Growth*. The course was under the jurisdiction of the School of World Mission faculty, since both the preoccupation with the demonic and the lack of medical resources in the Third World call for reliance on the supernatural to underscore the credibility of the gospel. Life on the frontiers of missions frequently puts Christ's servants in places where they confront the forces of evil and need a power beyond their own. To engage in such conflict with intellectual equipment or doctrine alone, as vital as that is, may not be sufficient. They need all that the Holy Spirit is for the challenge they wage against the secular pagan or demonic forces which seek to limit their effectiveness as Christians and to block the spreading of the gospel.

The course was designed to deal with both the theory and practice of the miraculous in the proclamation of the good news to non-Christian audiences. It was launched with considerable fanfare: for perhaps the only time in American church history an academic course preempted an entire issue of a national religious magazine—*Christian Life* (October, 1982). The fanfare at large was matched by ruffles and flourishes at home: the course broke all enrollment records at Fuller. Moreover, the laboratory sessions held at the close of each lecture drew overflow crowds of nonstudents who came to witness God's power. The School of World Mission professors were elated; the vast majority of students were grateful for the new insights into the works of God; Christian workers returning to their fields reported break-throughs in ministry; segments of the Seminary's constituency were thrilled by our obvious openness at Fuller to the exercise of gifts of power in the contemporary church. An advanced course, MC511, was added to the curriculum.

And so matters continued for a few years. Then questions which had probably been latent from the beginning of the course began to surface. Criticisms arrived from pastors whose student-interns had been indiscreet or rash in the application of what they had heard (or thought they heard) in the course. Faculty members were called to counsel students or members of their families when disillusionment followed their failure to experience the power of healing proclaimed in the classroom; a few persons were caught in a backlash of naïve attempts to discern demons. John Wimber—founder of the Vineyard movement and adjunct instructor along with C. Peter Wagner and Charles Kraft, our professors responsible for the course—came to be linked much more closely with Fuller in the minds of the public than his busy schedule of pastoral and conference ministry warranted; his audiences and readers were tempted to impute his opinions and approaches to our faculty more readily than the facts would support. Questions arose about the theological wisdom of conducting healing services in an academic rather than churchly setting. Eagerness to experience the works of the Spirit and to prepare our students to minister in deed as well as word short-circuited the signals of caution that usually prevail in a place like ours. In short, to borrow the language of another discipline, our engineering outran our science.

Prudently sensing the keen concern of colleagues in all three schools—Theology, Psychology and World Mission— the School of World Mission declared a moratorium on the course until the Seminary faculties could review the issues that had arisen and examine the biblical, theological, scientific, and pastoral implications of the curriculum. At that point, March 1986, our Provost, Dr. Lawrence DenBesten, appointed a task force, assigned it the agenda just described, and commissioned it to report its findings to him in the Fall of 1986. Dr. Den Besten's combination of medical expertise, missionary service in Nigeria, and theological perspective equipped him well for the leadership that he has given to this whole endeavor.

We have not disguised the fact that this book is the report of a task force. It is written as a statement of the findings and commitments of that diverse group. Its style, which smacks of the way in which faculty members approach serious questions, will give only temporary pause to thoughtful readers. Its subject matter wrestles aptly with the questions I listed at the beginning of this Foreword and with many others.

It is the crying need for such a study that prompts us to publish what might otherwise have remained an in-house document. The story of MC510 has had widespread circulation in the religious and secular media. We have had hundreds of inquiries from across the country about the reasons for the moratorium on the course and the possibility of its being scheduled in the future. One purpose of this book is to offer an update on our thinking and a public explanation for our decision to delay the teaching of the course.

A second, and more important, purpose of this release as a book is to share our theological and pastoral thinking with a larger audience of concerned Christians. What our task force has ventured, and what our faculty has received and affirmed, treats subjects of concern to thousands of pastors and tens of thousands of laypersons. The tack that it takes between the shoals of denying the possibility of miracles in our day and the rocks of presumption that demand miracles according to our need and schedule seems the way of wisdom for the entire church. The discussions of differences of world view and their bearing on how we view the supernatural will open new vistas for many. The survey of the ways in which the Creator may work his healing will enlarge our perspective on God and evoke our praises of his name. The thorny matter of the verification of claims to the miraculous is not bypassed; exuberance at the expense of truthfulness is shown to be no spiritual bargain. Finally the role of pain in Christian discipleship is explored, and the miracle of grace to bear pain is valued alongside the miracle of grace that eases pain.

The Seminary community is greatly indebted to the members of our faculty who committed themselves to this very sensitive task. We deeply appreciate the long hours they devoted to this assignment and are confident that a much larger audience of concerned persons will share our appreciation.

Each participant brought to the table his or her own academic and pastoral expertise and could have written extensively on some aspect of the issue. What the study represents is a distillation of their reflections and informed counsel as a committee. Their experience of drawing together from diverse positions and reaching the consensus reflected in the document was deeply moving and spiritually gratifying. The warmth and depth of that experience is part of the strength of their report and may serve as a model for the resolution of disagreement among thoughtful Christians.

I am more than grateful to the leadership of Dr. Lewis B. Smedes, Professor of Theology and Ethics, and member of the Christian Reformed Church, whose gracious and pastoral touch led these sensitive discussions to a fruitful and edifying conclusion and whose ready pen is largely responsible for the drafting. Other members of the committee included:

Dr. James E. Bradley, Associate Professor of Church History, (Foursquare)

Dr. Colin Brown, Professor of Systematic Theology (Episcopal)

Dr. Arthur Glasser, Dean Emeritus of the School of World Mission and Senior Professor of Theology and East Asian Studies (Associated Reformed Presbyterian)

Dr. Roberta Hestenes, Associate Professor of Christian Formation and Discipleship (Presbyterian Church U.S.A.)

Dr. Donald Hagner, Professor of New Testament (Presbyterian Church U.S.A.)

Dr. Paul Hiebert, Professor of Anthropology and South Asian Studies (Mennonite Brethren Church in North America)

Dr. H. Newton Malony, Professor of Psychology (United Methodist)

Dr. Samuel Southard, Professor of Pastoral Theology (Southern Baptist)

Dr. Russell Spittler, Associate Professor of New Testament (Assemblies of God)

Dr. Hendrika Vande Kemp, Associate Professor of Psychology (Presbyterian Church U.S.A.)

Dr. C. Peter Wagner, Donald A. McGavran Professor of Church Growth (Conservative Congregational Christian Conference).

Mr. Hugh James, Director of Communications and Public Affairs, contributed much to the process and Mr. Steven Pattie coordinated the composition and editing from beginning to end. Special thanks are due the editorial staff of Word, Inc., particularly Ernie Owen and Al Bryant, for the alacrity and enthusiasm with which they speeded the book into production.

The chairman and members of the Task Force would be the first to acknowledge the preliminary nature of their work. They offer no final solutions, no exhaustive answers. They have given us, rather, a set of pointers. I would like to think of this book as the first fruits of a harvest of discussion on these issues which are as crucial as they are delicate. The presence at Fuller of three schools each of which can make substantive contributions to the study of miracles and ministry bids well for future contributions. Our bridge-like role spanning the various wings of the church from historic protestant denominations to pentecostal and charismatic communions urges us to further investigation. And our newly founded David du Plessis Center for Christian Spirituality promises to be a vehicle not only for our own investigations but for those of other like-minded scholars who both bend before the majesty of God's ways and yearn to see his will done on earth as it is in heaven.

Advent, 1986   DAVID ALLAN HUBBARD

Pasadena, California

Preface

During recent years, healing ministries have become a celebrated component in the total ministry of the Christian church. It has been both an occasion for praising God and for asking questions. We at Fuller Theological Seminary celebrate with God's suffering people who have, through ministries of healing, been touched by God in ways that have brought healing to their bodies and assurance of God's reality to their hearts.

We who are called to educate men and women for ministry cannot, however, allow ourselves the luxury of uncritical appreciation. We owe it to the various churches and professional communities in which our graduates serve, as we owe it to our students and to Christ in whose service we are all engaged, to determine how we can and whether we ought to train men and women for ministry in the practice of healing. We must consider seriously what our specific academic role should be with respect to the ministry of miraculous healings.

The opportunity for reflection was offered to us when the practice of a healing ministry became integrated into a course taught in the Fuller curriculum. The opportunity became an obligation when, as the course was publicized in the religious and secular media, it tended to characterize Fuller Theological Seminary in the minds of many. But whether as an opportunity or an obligation, we undertook the task of examining the biblical, historical, theological, and pastoral implications of conducting sessions of healing in the context of a seminary course.

The Fuller faculty engaged in a forthright exchange of views and concerns. Our object was not to evaluate the phenomena of the miraculous in general, but to determine the propriety of its place in theological education. No one doubted that the occurrence of "signs and wonders" in the experience of the church merited the most careful and grateful study. We were sensitive to the special needs of missionaries to come to terms biblically with the phenomena of miraculous healings on the frontiers of the Christian mission. What was questioned by several was the place of scheduled sessions of healings in a Fuller classroom.

Our unfinished discussions prompted the appointment of a task force to address the question so that the entire faculty could measure its opinion in the light of its findings.

This document is the result. It does not in the least purport to be an exhaustive study of the phenomena of the miraculous, nor is it a critique of healing ministries. Rather, it is a reflection on the place of the miraculous within the seminary curriculum. It is more about the education of ministers, missionaries, and psychologists than it is about the ministry of healing. It was written for the Fuller faculty and whatever is said about the miraculous in general is set within the focus of a concern to teach responsibly.

We believe that the current enthusiastic interest in healing ministries is partly explained by a genuine passion in many of God's people for an experience of the reality of Jesus Christ in the sicknesses and sorrows of our present life. We are deeply sensitive to this passion; we share it. And it is because we too pray for, plan for, and train men and women for ministries in which the power of Christ is manifest that we accept the responsibility for the testing of our proper role in the ministry of miraculous healing.

1

The Coming of God's Kingdom and the Ministry of Healing

The Son of God came to earth as Healer and Savior of humankind. Joyfully and gratefully we praise him for becoming one of us, and for preaching the gospel while he was among us as Jesus of Nazareth. His word was one of good news to the poor and the captives, as well as for healing. Even a few dead people were raised to life, thus giving us signs of the ultimate and total healing he promises for all of God's children of the redeemed earth. We rejoice that the Spirit who enabled the healing Jesus is the Creator Spirit who sustains all of creation and works freely within the church to bring to believers of all times a foretaste of life, healed and restored, in the new creation to come. And we praise the Father who sent his Son to us; we praise him for his divine decision to redeem his creation through his Son and for his divine intention, through his Spirit, to heal his children totally—spiritually and physically, socially and individually.

All that we shall say rises from a grateful faith in the healing ministry of Christ and of his Holy Spirit.

As we listen to Scripture, our concern will be to seek an answer to two questions. First, does the gospel mandate or does it warrant the church to include miraculous healing as a regular and central feature of its public ministry? We may also state the first question this way: Are the instructions that Jesus gave to his disciples, to heal the sick and raise the dead, also his instructions to his ministers of all times and places? Second, does the Lord enjoin or encourage us to include the practice of miraculous healing in our curriculum, as we practice in the classroom the ministries of preaching and counseling?

We should say that if the Lord expects his church to perform miraculous healing as a regular and significant feature of its public ministry, it does not necessarily follow that theological seminaries are expected to include the practice of healing within the classroom. Not all that the church practices in ministry is appropriate within an academic setting. For instance, the Lord told the church to baptize people, and to partake of his body and blood, but this does not mean that it would necessarily be appropriate for a seminary to baptize people or serve holy communion in its classrooms.

Let us proceed, then, to consider several features of the biblical material. We provide only a summary survey of the relevant matters, but enough, we trust, to offer a biblical response to our question.

According to the Scriptures, Jesus Christ demonstrated the coming of God's rule among us by healing people from sickness and raising people from death. During the earliest days of his public ministry, we are told, "he healed many who were sick with various diseases, and cast out many demons" (Mark 1:34). With the touch of his hand, by the authority of his words, in the power of the Spirit, he opened the ears of the deaf and the mouths of the dumb, he sent the stream of life flowing through paralyzed legs, he set minds free from the demons that possessed them and, to the wonder of all who saw it, even brought a few persons from the realm of death back into mortal life. We who read the Gospels today are still, like Jesus' contemporaries, "astonished beyond measure" at his works, and are inclined to say with them, "He has done all things well . . ." (Mark 7:37).

Jesus also sent his disciples out with specific authority to heal people's sickness and even raise the dead (Matt. 10:1, 5–10). The Savior explained that the miraculous healings were a signal that the rule of God had broken into human life. Where God's kingdom comes, there human lives are healed. Salvation makes all things whole (Matt. 11:4, 5).

Since the rule of God has indeed come in Jesus Christ, should we not assume that the same healing miracles of his kingdom would be regularly performed in the ongoing ministry of the contemporary church? And should we not assume that when Jesus authorized his disciples to heal the sick and raise the dead he at the same time authorized all ministers of his church? And ought not a school that prepares men and women for ministry, by implication, be called to train them in the practice of performing miraculous healings in the power of God's Spirit?

In response to these questions, we invite a careful reading of the scriptural texts, and we call attention to a few features of the biblical witness to the coming of God's kingdom.

A. The Manifold Signs of God's Rule

The coming of God's kingdom is signaled by several acts in the ministry of Jesus. When John the Baptist's disciples came to him to inquire if he were the one or if they should look for another, he there and then, before their eyes, healed many of sickness, disease, blindness, and released them from evil spirits. Then he said, "Go back and report to John what you have seen and heard . . . . Blessed is the man who does not fall away on account of me" (Luke 7:18–23, NIV). Foremost among his works was his forgiving of people's sins, an act for which God alone had authority (Mark 2:7). He also preached the good news to the poor that their day of satisfaction had come (Matt. 11:5), to the captives that their day of liberation had come, to the slaves that their day of freedom had come (Luke 4:18), and to the blind that they would see. He made it clear that such good news signaled the advent of God's rule (Luke 4:18). And let us also remember the mighty works we hear of in the Virgin's prophecy of her divine Son's coming; she does not so much as mention temporary healings of individual bodies, but she speaks powerfully of the gifts of freedom to the oppressed, food to the hungry, power to the weak, and judgment on the proud (Luke 1:47–56). In short, her vision of the rule of God is one of righteousness, of justice, and of peace among men and women.

From these observations it is clear that miraculous healings and exorcisms are significant, though not the only signs of the coming of God's kingdom.

B. The Fragmentary Experience of the Kingdom of God in the World

The realization of his rule in the present time is a foretaste of its total triumph in another age. We still wait for "the new heavens and the new earth where righteousness dwells" (2 Peter 3:13) and where "righteousness and peace . . . kiss" (Psalm 85:10). We still long for the time when healing is whole and death is no more (Rev. 21:4). We pray the Lord's Prayer for God's good kingdom to come precisely because justice and peace have not yet embraced, the mourning of God's people still saddens our hearts, and the pain of disease still ravages the human body.

The New Testament warns against anticipating too much worldly benefit for the present time. Jesus himself told us that the call of the disciple is to a life of the cross, of self-denial, not to a life of reliance upon miracles to free us from the ailments and agonies that we are heir to on earth. The apostle Paul, in disputing with those who boasted of their power and wealth, called attention to his own quite different condition: "To the present hour we hunger and thirst, we are ill-clad and buffeted and homeless . . ." (1 Cor. 4:11). And yet, if not in a spectacular relief from pain and disability, then in a life of selfless love, the kingdom of God exists in power among us (1 Cor. 4:20).

C. The "Signs and Wonders" of the Kingdom

The Gospel of John uses the word "signs" for Jesus' wonderful works (John 2:11, 18, 23, etc.), proclaiming thereby that Jesus' works were indicators of God's powerful healing presence. At Pentecost, the apostle Peter recalled that Jesus was "attested . . . by God with mighty works and wonders and signs which God did through him in your midst" (Acts 2:22–24). Those who watched were awestruck as the apostles themselves did "many wonders and signs" in Christ's name (Acts 2:43). And, in keeping with the expectation that God would "perform miraculous signs and wonders" (Acts 4:29, 30, NIV), the apostles themselves went on to perform "many miraculous signs and wonders among the people" (Acts 5:12, NIV).

Thus, clearly, "signs and wonders" were done both by Jesus and the apostles. But what does this fact tell us about the church's ministry today and about the propriety of training present-day ministers in the doing of "signs and wonders" in the name of Jesus?

We should note, first, that in the biblical context "signs and wonders" have a specific connotation. There is a categorical uniqueness about them; they have a narrow, though radically important function within a narrow, though redemptively crucial history. They signal, not just anything that surprises and awes us, but God's decisive actions for the salvation of the world. They are signals that the kingdom is drawing near. They are harbingers of the advent of Christ. The phrase "signs and wonders" is biblical language for the revelatory events of a salvation history that had its climax in the incarnation, death, resurrection, and advent of the Spirit, leading to the birth of the Christian church.

Therefore, when we pray for the healing of God's suffering

children, and when he answers our prayers, we may best honor the unique acts of God in Jesus if we do not speak of answers to our prayers for healing as "signs and wonders."

We should also observe that Jesus, while performing miracles, was critical of people's hankering after signs and wonders. "An evil and adulterous generation [that] seeks for a sign" (Matt. 12:39; 16:4), Jesus said, and even when it was just a natural desire for tangible evidence of his messianic credibility, he regretted any demand for signs (cf. Luke 11:16 and John 4:48). The apostle Paul, in the same spirit, identified a desire for signs as characteristic, not of Christian faith, but of the skeptical among the Jews (1 Cor. 1:22).

We may also note this: the fact that someone does "signs and wonders" is not a self-evident indicator that God is healingly at work. In fact, the wonder-worker may be working against God. We remember the magicians of Pharaoh who matched wonder with wonder in their contest with Moses. And we recall the caveat of Moses that a prophet could come and do "a sign or a wonder" in order to seduce the people away from their calling to love God and walk in his commandments (Deut. 13:1–5). And we recall that Jesus himself warned of false Christs who would "show great signs and wonders" that could lead the elect astray (Matt. 24:24). And, as all readers of the apostle Paul know, he predicted that the anti-Christ would come on stage with spectacular "signs and wonders" (2 Thess. 2:9).

All of this serves to remind us that the occurrence of "signs and wonders" invites us, not to unquestioning credulity, but very specifically to a critical examination in light of the whole will of God for his church.

The ministry of the church must take great care to insure that any public practice of healing does not cater to an immature expectation that the power of God's kingdom manifests itself primarily in temporary though miraculous relief of occasional sickness and pain. The minister of the gospel should major in the power that enables ordinary people to bear the cross and accept the burdens of suffering for the sake of doing God's will in a world that hungers for forgiveness, reconciliation, justice, peace, the feeding of the hungry, and the relief of the oppressed.

D. Our Lord's Mandate to the Disciples

Jesus sent his disciples out with authority to heal people's sicknesses, to cleanse lepers, to cast out demons, and even to raise the dead (Matt. 10:1, 5–10; Mark 6:7–13; Luke 9:1–6). A second mission of some seventy disciples is reported in Luke 10:1–20.

Is Jesus' mandate to the disciples a mandate for the Christian church of all ages? Did he, in commissioning his disciples, commission the church, in every time, to heal the sick and raise the dead? And, if so, is it as central to the church's contemporary witness as it was to the witness of the disciples?

Some among us interpret the Lord's directives to his disciples as equivalent to a mandate to all successors of the disciples, that is, to the church of all times and places to come. There is a certain reasonableness to this interpretation. The all-embracing kingdom had come in Jesus; its healing power sweeps beyond the borders of Judea to any place where his name is preached and believed and obeyed. And since Jesus was commissioning his disciples to preach the good news that the kingdom had arrived and to do the works that manifest its coming, why should not those same directives apply to all who are called to preach the same good news?

By way of response, we must first note that the specific mission under consideration had limited objectives. Its objective was to prepare the way for Jesus' coming to those specific parts of the country. In keeping with their limited objectives, the disciples were not to carry any provisions, nor any money. Later, when conditions were different, Jesus gave different directions (Luke 22:35, 36), indicating again that, at this time, his commissionings were not general, timeless mandates, but specific and limited mandates for specific occasions.

Secondly, after his resurrection, Jesus—according to the most ancient Greek texts—gives no mandate to undertake a healing ministry. He does tell his disciples to teach all nations and to baptize in his name (Matt. 28:19, 20). He does speak of repentance and forgiveness being preached to all nations (Luke 24:47). He does promise the authority of the Spirit to forgive and retain sins (John 20:22, 23). But he does not reinvest his disciples with a commission to do miraculous healing and resuscitation.

The disciples, as we have noted, performed "signs and wonders" immediately after Pentecost. They witnessed, no doubt, to the advent of the Spirit of Christ, just as they had witnessed to the advent of the Savior. And though, as time went on, gifts of healing became subordinate to moral and spiritual transformation, the apostle Paul still mentions them with thanksgiving. True, he stresses even more the sufficiency of grace to bear redemptively with one's thorns and crosses, but he continues to acknowledge the gifts of healing (1 Cor. 12:9) and prophecy (1 Thess. 5:20).

Indications are, then, that Jesus' instructions to his disciples to prepare his way to the "lost sheep of the house of Israel" are not the same as his instructions to his universal church. The disciples' mandate to heal the sick and raise the dead is not necessarily equivalent to the church's mandate.

We in no way mean to discourage the ministers of the church from praying believingly for sick people to be healed, whether miraculously or through the normal processes God provides for healing. We believe in the healing efficacy of prayer. We rejoice with those who have been given the grace of healing, be it ever so temporary. However, many of us would say that the church at large was not commissioned to heal the sick and raise the dead, and that when Jesus sent his disciples on a special mission to heal the sick and raise the dead (Matt. 10, Luke 10), he did not commission the church to do the same.

Jesus did, however, promise that believers would do the works that he did and even greater works (John 14:12–14). But what did he mean? We cannot help noticing that none of the disciples copied all of Jesus' miracles. None of them walked on water. None of them fed five thousand people out of a basketful of food. Together, they did not perform as many miracles as Jesus did. And, in any case, they could hardly have topped a miracle like the resurrection of Lazarus. How, then, did they, and how may we, do "greater works" than Jesus did?

We cannot say for sure what Jesus meant. We note that, compared by any ordinary standard of equivalence, the healings reported by contemporary healing ministries hardly qualify as "greater works" than Jesus did. But we may well believe that the total scope of healing in all the medical and psychiatric hospitals, sanatoria, clinics, and other institutions that Christian believers have been enabled by the Spirit to build and operate around the world probably have indeed brought about countless times as many healings as our Lord performed during his brief sojourn with us on earth. And it may also be true that spiritually motivated movements of social reform have improved the living conditions of people to a quantitative degree far greater than the occasional physical healings our Lord performed as testimonies to his messianic office. So, in terms of effects on the earthly lives of people, the believing community has, without claim to the miraculous, done "greater works" than Jesus did.

In promising "greater works than these," Jesus may also have been putting a higher value on the spiritual effects of what the church would do than he did on his own miraculous healings of bodies that, in any case, got terminally sick again, and died. He promised his disciples that their witness would bear fruit unto eternal life (see John 5:20; 6:28f; 16:7–11; 20:22, 23). He promised, through the Virgin Mary, that the hungry would be given food to eat, the lowly would be lifted up, and the unrighteous powerful and rich would be scattered and sent away empty (Luke 1:47–53). It may have been in such senses as these, that his disciples were to do greater works than Jesus.

E. Healings in the Apostolic Church

With the immediate impact of Pentecost, disciples did things that Luke called "signs and wonders." Should we understand this fact as an indication that the church of Christ ever after must set "signs and wonders" high on its agenda for ministry?

We must note that only a small minority of those baptized by the Spirit, the apostles Peter and Paul, and possibly a few others, did miraculous works. In the Pauline letters, miraculous healing is, far from being a center-stage preoccupation, hardly evident. The working of miracles gets passing attention in Galatians 3:5 and 1 Corinthians 12:9ff, after which it does not appear on Paul's apostolic agenda. In fact, if we read only the Pauline epistles, we would likely assume that the life of the Christian, far from promising instant healing of physical ailments, offers a pilgrimage into suffering for the sake of Christ—with a hope of complete and permanent healing in the life to come. It is the revolutionary gospel of justification by faith, the call to sanctification and service, and the resurrection hope that impassions the apostolic ministry of St. Paul.

The apostle James, however, gives specific instruction to the church about prayers for the sick. "Is any among you suffering? Let him call for the elders of the church, and let them pray over him, anointing him with oil in the name of the Lord; and the prayer of faith will save the sick man, and the Lord will raise him up; and if he has committed sins, he will be forgiven" (James 5:13–15).

Clearly, James does not give us a scenario for public healing services. We seem to have a case where a person is too ill to attend the regular worship service, so the elders are, quietly and without advertisement, to go to his or her bedside for anointing and prayers. The rite is prescribed only for members of the church; no public invitation is given indiscriminately to the sick and afflicted of the world. There is an ancient view that the sick ministered to were actually dying, that the anointing is a kind of last rite, and that the promise of the Lord's raising of the sick person refers to the perfect and permanent healing that comes with life after death, and eventually with resurrection. In any case, what James specifically does not prescribe is a public ministry in which physical healings are a normal public feature.

What conclusions can we draw from this brief survey of the ministry of Jesus and his disciples at the dawn of God's coming to redeem his people and establish his kingdom?

1. The ministry of the church is continuous with, but not identical to, the ministry of Jesus and his disciples. Certain parts of the disciples' work were focused specifically on the coming of Jesus and his Spirit.

2. The power within the church to perform its ministry is the same power given to the disciples in the times of Jesus and the early church.

3. There is reason to doubt that the temporary commission that Jesus gave his disciples in Matthew 10 is a permanent mandate for the churches.

4. Prayers for healing are essential to the church's ministry, though miraculous healing of the sick and the raising of the dead are not indicated as primary features of the church's public ministry.

5. Gifts of healings and miracles, just as gifts of healing and prophecy, are part of the life of the body of Christ today and should be used, under the guidance of the Holy Spirit and the instruction of the Scriptures.

6. The life of the church, while it waits for the coming of the wholly new earth where Christ will reign as Lord, is characterized as a life of saving faith, of patient hope, and forgiving love, as well as a place where we may expect healing from pain and disability.

We conclude this chapter as we began it, with praise to the Lord for his ministry of healing, a total healing that includes the body as well as the mind and the spirit, and the community as well as individuals. It promises to restore all of life in all its parts to the fullness of health and wholeness, as he had meant it from the beginning. We give thanks that the ministry of the church participates in his ministry of power to reconcile estranged people, to bring a foretaste of the time when justice and peace shall be married forever, and to heal the bodies of people who are sick. Wherever his power is felt on earth, we rejoice and give him thanks.

2

The Faith and Practice of the Early Church

What post-apostolic Christians believed and did about miraculous healing is of more than historical interest to us, even though it is less than normative. We should therefore make at least some cursory observations about the faith and practices of the churches in the two or three centuries following the close of the canon.

The Christians of the second and third centuries expected miracles to occur in the lives of believers. The church fathers considered their generations to be in direct continuity with the primitive church. In fact, the subject of demons and exorcism is more prominent in the post-apostolic church than in the church of the New Testament. It is, of course, within neither our interest nor our competence to determine the validity of the reports of miracles, but only to examine the fathers' beliefs and attitudes toward them.

During the time of the Apostolic Fathers the gift of prophecy was more prominent than the gifts of healing. Nonetheless, we find in Justin Martyr, for example, as well as in Irenaeus, that gifts of healing were acknowledged, even reporting resurrections of dead people. In the same vein, both Tertullian and Cyprian testified to the presence of the gift of prophecy, or visions, and the gifts of healing and exorcism in north Africa. Origen said that he himself had seen cures performed by Christians in the power of the Holy Spirit: we have seen, he writes, "many delivered from serious ailments, and from mental distraction and madness, and countless other diseases, which neither men nor demons had cured."

While it is sometimes observed that the phenomena of the miraculous declined in the last half of the third century, we have solid evidence that various liturgies still included prayers for healing. In the *Sacramentary of Serapion,* for example, we find this prayer:

> Lord God of compassion, stretch out your hand and graciously grant *(charisai)* all the sick to be healed, *graciously* grant them to be considered worthy of health, release *(appallaxon)* them from the sickness which lies upon them, in the name of your only son let them be healed, let his holy name be to them a medicine *(pharmakon)* for health and wholeness . . . Amen.

The blessing of oil to be used in anointing the sick and in the practice of exorcism can also be documented from early liturgies. The gifts of healing were prayed for in certain ordination ceremonies, as we observe in both the *Constitutions Apostololicae* and the *Canons of Hippolytus.*

We can be sure that belief in miracles was widespread geographically; prominent church leaders in Asia Minor, southern Gaul, north Africa, Egypt, and Rome all attest to the conviction that miracles were part of the legacy of the primitive church. Not everyone exercised the gifts, and pagan magicians claimed the same powers as did Christians. But, carefully monitored by the leadership of the church, the gifts were not uncommonly practiced in the church.

Thus, without evaluating the accuracy of the reports, we know beyond doubt that the church fathers of the second and third centuries believed in and expected miracles of healing, and that many were reported to have happened.

With this in mind, we will review the setting for the early church fathers' belief in miracles in order better to evaluate their perspective on the miraculous.

The first thing we should say about the setting is that the possibility of miraculous healing was seen in the framework of a life of suffering and dying. Justin Martyr, for example, reminded believers that any temporary relief from suffering that miraculous healing might bring did not exempt them from the life of suffering and even death that following Christ might lead them to. The gift of prophecy was often used to encourage people in the face of possible martyrdom.

The true power of the gospel, said Justin Martyr, was seen in the willingness of Christians to die for Christ. And, as for verification of the gospel, the fathers saw it in the suffering of Christians more than in physical healing. Church growth, said Tertullian, came from the blood of the martyrs, as well as from miraculous healings. Pagans could and did compete with Christians' miracles; they could not compete with their readiness to die for their faith.

The second thing we may observe is that for the fathers, moral renewal was at least as prominent a demonstration of the gospel's power as healing. In the same texts that discuss miracles, the quality of Christian character is held up as primary testimony to the truth. Anthanasius, to mention only one, cites exorcism as a sign of the gospel's truth, but in the same breath he mentions the moral quality of the Christians' life: "so that the adulterer no longer commits adultery, and the murderer murders no more, nor is the inflictor of wrong any longer grasping, and the profane is henceforth religious." The same writers who stressed the apologetic force of miracles—notably Ignatius, Tertullian, and Origen—made much of the miracle of a transformed life.

The third thing we observe is that the fathers were concerned about the ethical aspect of the miraculous itself.

They wanted to keep the works of the Spirit clearly separate from the wonders of pagan magic. They paid close attention to probing the nature of reported miracles to determine their authenticity, not fearing that a critical concern might discourage genuine faith.

A fourth observation is that the fathers were very sensitive to the seductions of spiritual power. Vanity was recognized as a real temptation; but the worst lure was money, and anyone repeatedly asking for money was likely to be labeled a false prophet.

In sum, the church fathers of the second and third centuries give a clear witness to the early church's faith in the healing power of the Spirit and the healing gifts enjoyed by some Christians. There is evidence that though the early church did on occasion sensationalize the miraculous it did not see it as the central or climactic evidence of the power of God in human life. The miraculous was subordinate to the moral, the healing of bodies to the renewing of lives, and any gift of healing for the moment was accepted in awareness that the follower of the Cross might suffer and die as a Christian.

Stories of miraculous healings and exorcisms were even more prominent in the fourth and fifth centuries than they were in the first three. Increasingly, however, with the cessation of persecution, attention focused upon the relics of the martyrs as the instruments of healing. The element of critical discernment found in the pre-Nicene church was often less evident, and the masses who came into the church sometimes failed to distinguish between Christ and their former carnival gods.

The Protestant Reformers rejected most of the accoutrements surrounding miracles, including the intercession of the saints, and the manipulation of relics and shrines. But they did not abandon all sense of the supernatural in daily life. Luther himself had wracking experiences with the devil on separate occasions. At times when people were extremely oppressed by a sense of Satan, he prescribed the ministry of two or three good people, the laying on of hands, and prayer in Christ's name. John Wesley, too, on occasion, ministered to people who were in conflict with the devil by calling special and extended periods of intercession.

We shall not dwell here on the gruesome witch hunts of New England where Christian sense of the supernatural ran amuck in obsessive fear and cruel torture. In any case, while the Reformation brought back the sobriety of the second and third centuries, it did not disallow the possibility of God's miraculous intervention.

From all this we can draw only the most modest conclusion. We see that some Christian expectation of miraculous divine intervention in life existed almost continuously from the time of the apostles to the Reformation. We also observe that this expectation, when separated from the context of suffering, led rather easily from a sober and responsible faith to superstition and exploitation, from liturgical prayer to quasi-magical tricks. The Reformers of the church believed that preoccupation with miracles seduced believers from the heart of the gospel's spiritual message and moral mandate, and they returned the churches to the heart of the matter, justifying faith and sanctifying obedience.

3

Our Views of God and His World

Our belief in, and our expectations of the miraculous power of God in our lives, depend to a large extent on how we view the environment within which human life is nourished, protected, and threatened. Do we live as persons within an environment that is thoroughly impersonal, where all that happens is determined by natural causes without influence from a transcendent spirit? Or do we live in an environment that is constantly open to God's presence and subject to his power? How do we view the world we live in and the world that lives in us?

We all learn to fit the pieces of our world together into some pattern that helps us know what we can expect from it, what we can do to manipulate it to our benefit, how we can adjust new things into it, and most crucially, how it all relates to powers and persons beyond or beneath it. Our patterns of the world as we experience and understand it become what we often call paradigms for making sense out of life in the world.

We fit the new fragments of reality as we perceive and experience them into our paradigms; and we assume that we have understood them when they fit into our accustomed way of viewing reality. But now and then we encounter pieces of reality that our paradigms do not have a place for. This happened when things Einstein perceived about the movement of objects in space did not fit the paradigm that most people accepted on the basis of Newton's mechanical view of the world. Newton had led most people in the West to see the world as something like a clock where all the pieces were linked together as in an infinite system of gears and springs. But Einstein discovered huge pieces of reality that did not fit together at all like the predictable works of a clock. So, we had to make a choice: we had to deny Einstein's perceptions or draw a new picture and create a new paradigm of reality into which his perceptions could fit. Most of us repainted our picture. Or, we make what is called a "paradigm-shift."

There are paradigms of reality that are, so far as natural causes and effects are concerned, essentially godless. They construe the universe as a magnificent nexus of physical causes and effects, a world where all things are and all events occur only because of physical antecedents that can be located, identified, and possibly manipulated by the interjection of other physical influences. Variations of these paradigms allow for an influence on the physical world by mind or human spirit but not by God or Satan. In all variations of the godless world-view God is eliminated from effective presence in creation, grace is separated from nature, and the power of the Spirit is irrelevant to the power of nature. This is the paradigm of unbelief. We reject it.

Missiologists, with good reason, have alerted us to the possibility that, notwithstanding their theological denial of the godless world-view, Christians may inadvertently adopt its pragmatic premises. We do well to heed those missiologists who express fears that many Christians in the Western world have capitulated to the naturalistic and technological paradigms of modern Western culture. We know the temptation to reduce the activity of God in the world to our emotions and our morals and to an awakening of faith in forgiveness and hope for heaven. It is tempting to accept the secular hypothesis that all physical reality has only physical cause, and thus to surrender all expectations of healing incursions of God's kingdom into our disease-ridden world, to surrender them all to the shrunken, shriveled, and static paradigm of myopic secularism.

We intend to resist this temptation.

Missionaries frequently report the challenge of their encounter with world-views that are totally hospitable to the Gospel accounts of the miracles of healing performed by Jesus and his disciples. Their paradigms of reality are wide open to the presence and power of benign and hostile spirits who bring the good and the bad things we experience in life. So when they hear talk of the miracles done by Jesus, what they hear fits into their paradigm beautifully. And they expect that if Jesus is the Christ, and if his Spirit is the Spirit of God, he will heal the sick and release people from demons today just as he did in the villages of Judea and the countryside of Galilee.

Christians of the Western world, some missiologists tell us, need to make a paradigm shift so that, like the people innocent of Newtonian physics, they too can welcome the miraculous works of Jesus into their lives, and into the lives of people to whom they witness of Christ. We are not likely to open our lives to the "signs and wonders" of the Spirit, these missiologists tell us, unless we modify our world-view enough to allow God a place in the physical world so he can touch and heal human lives where they are broken and diseased.

We welcome this missiological challenge, for, as Christian believers, we must be ready to turn our world-views on their heads if they cannot accommodate the reality and power of God within natural and human life. And if we have doubts and questions about miraculous ministries of healing, it is our responsibility to examine anew our ways of viewing God's world. Only then will we know whether our doubts arise from a secret surrender to the seductions of secular paradigms of reality.

But we should also be careful not to buy too quickly into world-views that we meet in non-Western cultures simply on grounds that they are more hospitable to miracles than is our world-view. Readiness for signs and wonders is not the only criterion for a Christian world-view.

We should not rush to the premise that modern Christians have two world-views to choose between. The one world-view represents a naturalistic, god-evacuated world in which all things that happen are locked into a cause-effect nexus that is energized only by natural forces; the other is presented as a supernaturalistic, spirit-populated world in which most things that happen are brought about, whimsically and arbitrarily, by spirits who cause good and bad things to happen. Surely our options are not exhausted by the rationalistic, godless paradigm and the irrational, supernaturalistic paradigm.

We believe that there is a world-view more true to the Scriptures than the spiritualistic, primitive world-view in which transcendent spirits are frequent but erratic invaders. This world-view is also more true than the naturalistic, secular world-view from which God is, for all practical purposes, excluded.

We may pause here, before sketching the most distinctive features of the biblical world-view, to observe that the term world-view is used with more than one focus. Sometimes we speak of world-view as a way of interpreting the ultimate truth about the cosmos, its origin, its purpose, its destiny. At other times, we speak of world-view as a way of interpreting the forces that are at work in and on human lives, forces with which we must come to terms, must control or exploit or otherwise manipulate in order to flourish or survive among them.

The two meanings overlap, of course, and how we see our world on the deepest level influences our view of it on a more immediate and practical level. But, as we use the word *world-view* here, we will be thinking primarily of the categories by means of which we make sense of the realities that impact our earthly lives for weal or woe. This is the level at which world-views shape human life in cultures not dominated by rationalism and technology, the level at which the Christian gospel is most pragmatically challenged.

When we talk of our view of the world, we talk inevitably of our view of God. Our world-view is the echo of our God-view. And our God-view shapes and forms our world-view. As we go on to speak of our understanding of the biblical God-view and world-view we are prepared to change it—to "shift our paradigm"—if it is shown by any degree to be a capitulation to either the secular or the spiritist paradigm.

We may begin by affirming that we view our world as a God-permeated cosmos. The God above all things is present with power in every dimension, material or mental, physical or spiritual, of our universe. The transcendent God is also the intangible energy behind all tangible energies, the cause of all natural causes. His Spirit is active, creating and preserving human life, replenishing its power to resist the negative forces of decay and disease and endlessly weaving the fabric of living cells. He gives life to the fragile flesh of his children.

He moves every being toward its unique end. He provides all that creatures receive to nourish and sustain their lives; he is nature's secret healer, the mysterious power within nature to overcome its ever-present enemy, death.

Every genuine healing can be a sign. Every healed wound may be a wonder. Every experience of restored vitality and health may be a signal that God is present and at work in his world. Ordinary healings are no less divine than miraculous healings.

Since he is the healing energy within every personal or technological healing agent, it is appropriate to thank God for the healing of every disease. We thank him for the remission of cancer; we thank him for the relief of a headache. We thank him for the healing of depressed spirits and broken limbs. We thank him for a successful excision of a malignant tumor and for the gift of a transplanted kidney. And we thank him for those inexplicable healings we call miracles. We who see God *in* all genuine healing thank him *for* all genuine healing.

If we affirm that God is everywhere, we also affirm that he is somewhere in particular. If we affirm that God is the deepest cause of all healing, we affirm that he may be the miraculous cause of any particular healing. If we meet him at every corner, why should we be surprised to meet him at the next corner?

We wish, in this general way, to stress that the world, seen through biblical lenses, is a God-permeated world. We do not live in a universe that is normally God-free; ours is not a universe whose wondrous regularity and predictability is the accidental effect of natural forces exercising themselves mindlessly for millions of years. Nor do we live in a world that is normally godless and free, but is invaded now and then, here and there, by supernatural beings who either arbitrarily assault, or whimsically heal, human life. Nor do we believe in a God who created the world and then left it to its own magnificent devices, except when he, on call, responds to repair the occasional damage done by alien spirits. In such a world, we would be able to see God *only* in the miraculous, the extraordinary, the irregular, in encounters between him and the evil spirits.

In the biblical view his children can see him everywhere and in everything. And those who see him from the biblical vista thank and praise him for the healing flow of his tender mercies through all the valleys of their fragile lives. "Thou sendest forth thy Spirit, they are created; and thou renewest the face of the ground" (Psalm 104:30, KJV).

The presence of God is an ordered and ordering presence. As he formed the world, so he also keeps forming it; as he once ordered it, he keeps ordering it. He is the creative bulwark against spiritual disorder, moral chaos, and physical disease. He moves through his fluid creation in accustomed ways, moves so regularly that we can speak of his creative paths as natural laws. What we call the laws of nature are laws, notations of predictability, only because the God of creation continuously orders as he upholds his creation.

Having affirmed, as a basic component of the biblical world-view, that God is immanent as an ordering and healing presence within the physical world, we must also take note of that awesome disturbance called the Fall. We admit that we cannot measure the depths nor describe the processes by which human choice against the Creator disturbed the order of physical nature. But we know from the biblical record, that this human choice had tragic repercussions beyond the soul and its private relationship with God. Somehow, the delicate genetic rhythms were interrupted, the fragile balances of reciprocating ecological influences were skewed, the sensitive mutuality of mind and body was broken, and all that moved and ordered life toward vigor and health was inhibited and disturbed. Sin took a cosmic toll.

The ancient Antagonist of heaven became an alien presence within the veins and arteries of earth. The Enemy above invaded God's creation below, and transcendent hostility became imminent insurgency. Seducing the minds and hearts of individual persons, captivating the political powers and corrupting political systems, the Enemy also insinuated his debilitating touch into the ecosystems of nature and the biosystems of the human body.

Yet, the Creator was not undone by the Alien; our Father's world did not become the Enemy's empire. The earth was invaded, but it was not possessed by the demonic. God is ruler yet. Demons are not lords; they are formidable, but they are not sovereign. The earth is the Lord's, he made it, sustains it, and guards it against the futile and sometimes grandiose assaults of his Enemy.

When God came to earth in Jesus Christ, he came "unto his own"—his own people, but his own world as well. And when he delivered his people from the effects of sin, he also reaffirmed his claim on the earth that he had made to be their home. His incarnation, his cross, and his resurrection undid the Enemy and rescued our lives, minds, and bodies from the Interloper's debilitating grasp. We look forward now, not only to personal freedom and wholeness, but to a new and redeemed earth where everything, in persons and systems, and in minds and bodies, is right again. The God who is in, under, over, and around every nucleus of every atom has invested his world in the risen Christ and made him Lord of all things, now and in times to come, and is leading his family to its ultimate and total healing.

It is pertinent that, insidiously corruptive as the effects of the Fall were, they did not change the fundamental focus of the biblical world-view: the earth was, is, and shall be the Lord's, from the molecular mysteries of DNA to the cosmic constellations of worlds in space. And it is equally pertinent that the great miracles of incarnation and resurrection did not violate or change the ordered and ordering work of God in nature; they only have begun to release nature from the temporary disturbance of its would-be Destroyer.

We still wrestle, as the apostle Paul says, against principalities and powers, and we still confront them in oppressive corruption of political powers, in the deceits and lusts of individuals and in the prevailing presence of death. But we are on the Lord's side. And because he is Lord of all, we can, with truth, righteousness, and the gospel of peace "quench all the flaming darts of the evil one" (Eph. 6:16).

From all that has been said we can conclude that the normal and most fruitful way to combat the disordering effects of evil in nature is to cooperate with nature's ordering processes, its creative and healing energies, along with the potentials within mind and spirit for health-restoring influences on the body. To release the healing powers of creation is to work with creation's Redeemer and against alien disorder, debilitation, and death. It is fundamental to all our resistance to disorder and disease in human life that the Savior is the Creator, the transcendent Lord of spirits is the imminent Lord of nature, and the Spirit of Jesus Christ is the Creator Spirit in whom and through whom all flesh flourishes in its fragile but fantastic beauty.

It is God's presence as the designing Sustainer that makes possible the work of medical science and the healing arts. It is his ordering that makes it possible to diagnose illness and give a credible prognosis of its course. It is his ordering presence that turns surgical skill into healing art. In and around and under the benefits of medical research and the healing arts is the sustaining, ordering, healing presence of the Creator and Redeemer of all things.

Thus medical science and the healing arts do not need to deny the presence of God as a premise for affirming the order of nature. And the believing physician does not need to deny the order of nature as a premise for acknowledging God as the ordering Physician. Indeed, the omnipresence of the ordering God is the bedrock of faith in an ordered nature. For the medical scientist, physician, or psychologist, the stable regularity of nature is a presumption of both medical science and the healing arts. God's dynamic ordering of nature is the precondition of that ordered nature.

We thus reject any world-picture in which God only occasionally invades the world via some interstices of nature or through some gaps unfilled by natural processes, to work an occasional miracle. We reject any script for the world in which God only now and then breaks through the hard crust of alien nature, overcomes its impersonal laws, and rescues isolated individuals from disease-bearing demons.

We reject these views, not because they make too much of God's occasional demonstration of power, but because they make too little of God's constant presence and power.

In the biblical view, a miracle is a signal that God is, for a moment and for a special purpose, walking down paths he does not usually walk. A miracle is not a sign that a God who is usually absent is, for the moment, present. It is only a sign that God who is always present in creative power is working here and now in an unfamiliar style.

This brief sketch of one feature of the biblical world-view can only hint at the fuller picture on a broader canvas that Christian philosophers and theologians must paint for us. But it is enough, perhaps, for us to draw from it a few implications for the training of ministers to be agents of healing in our world.

We who are called to educate men and women for ministry must help them draw biblical paradigms of God's way of working in the world and to discern appropriate ways in which they may be agents of his healing power. We do not prepare them to minister to people in a world where God is either absent or, if present, relevant only to pious imagination and feelings. Neither do we prepare them to minister in a world where God's presence and power is known only in the miraculous or the spectacular. We prepare them to be aware of the possibility of demonic influences in human life and human systems. But we also prepare them to minister to people in ways that open their minds and hearts to the presence of God in the ordered world of medicine where technology is his visible hand and where physicians are his healing servants.

We want to encourage students to be disposed toward belief in and readiness to receive miracles and to be men and women who publicly pray for the healing of stricken people. But we do not prepare them for ministries that focus centrally on the possibility that God may on occasion walk the less traveled road of miracles. And we want to prepare them to minister wisely to people who were encouraged to pray for and expect miracles, only to learn that for them God does not walk the road less traveled, that their diseases follow predictable paths, and who are left in doubt and confusion about the apparently arbitrary ways of a God who promised so much, but left them out in the cold.

We must help students for ministry to see, through the

lenses of faith, that every brush stroke in our picture of the world has the hue of divinity. We must encourage them to see God in the orderly, as well as the unusual ways of nature, so that they are spiritually equipped to help God's people rejoice that every genuine healing is divine healing, every surge of health is a hint of his presence, every vital impulse is a creative nudge from the Creator's hand, that every breath of life we breathe is the animation of his Spirit and that on our human pilgrimage, we walk in stride with God.

4

The Place of Suffering
in Christian Experience

It is appropriate that a discussion of the ministry of healing should include some biblical observations on suffering in the Christian life. As we ask whether it is appropriate to train ministers in the practice of miraculous relief from suffering, we should ask about training ministers to lead people in the redemptive acceptance of suffering.

We believe that suffering is compatible with faithful Christian living, and that some suffering should be expected in anyone's pilgrimage. We do not believe that Christian believers have a special entitlement to lasting health and instant healing. The Bible indicates that suffering is an inescapable component of, and not the exception, in the Christian life. Therefore, we reject any suggestion that believers have a blank check from God that offers them certain healing from sickness and handicaps if only their faith is strong enough. On the contrary, we believe that suffering is an inescapable ingredient of, and not the exception in, Christian living.

When miraculous healing becomes the cutting edge of faith, people ask: "Why should we suffer?" When discipleship becomes the cutting edge of faith, we ask: "How can we turn our suffering to the service of our neighbor, to our own growth, and to the glory of God?" Recall what suffering is. Suffering is the experience of any condition one most sorely wishes were absent. It may be the experience of physical or spiritual pain; it may be the loss of something very precious to one's life. It may be subjection to alcoholism or drugs. It may also be our empathetic participation in the suffering of others, near to us or far away. Whatever the condition, if one desperately wishes to be relieved of it, he or she suffers.

By definition, suffering entails putting up with anything we would rather avoid. This is why popular interest in miraculous relief from suffering is so understandable; it is in the nature of suffering for us to wish to be healed of it. To want God to relieve suffering is natural and expectable for any believer. If we believe that God wills our well-being and if we devoutly wish to be well, why should we not ask a loving God to relieve us? And when he does not relieve us, we suffer the more. Sometimes we suffer doubly, precisely because of our disappointment that God does not remove the cause of our suffering.

But the Bible has its own ways of looking at suffering.

For one thing, it teaches us that by God's grace, we can bear with hope and patience the suffering we experience as the price for living as vulnerable and imperfect physical creatures.

Some of our suffering comes with the privilege of being alive as sensitive beings in bodies that are prey to disease, accident, and stress. Some of our suffering comes from the malice of mean spirits and the carelessness of bungling neighbors. And sometimes we suffer as the consequence of our own sins and stupidity. With respect to all such suffering, Christians live in patient hope for the ultimate relief of God's children from all the ills to which sinful and fragile flesh is heir. And we live with the possibility of discovering that God's grace is sufficient for us while we wait.

The Bible also reminds us that the Christian may at times have to suffer simply because he or she is faithful to Christ in

times hostile to the gospel and among people who are ene-
mies of Christ. The Cross is the inescapable symbol for the
Christian lifestyle, the reality that shadows all of our human
pretensions and expectations. Paul gives us due warning that
we may suffer for Christ's sake (Phil. 1:29) and that it is of
highest importance for us to know Christ and to share his
suffering. But he also showed the world that it was possible
even to "rejoice in . . . suffering" (Col. 1:24).

Thus, faith is not an entree into a life without suffering.
Even if we are not persecuted for following Christ, we are
called to share the suffering of others who suffer for any
reason. Jesus identified himself with prisoners, with sick
people, hungry and thirsty people, and told us that when we
involve our lives with their suffering we do it unto him
(Matt. 25:40). When Paul warns us that we cannot be the
grateful heirs of Christ's glory unless we suffer with Christ
(Rom. 8:17), he doubtless includes empathetic suffering
with the Body of Christ.

Thus, whether we suffer from natural and human causes,
suffer because of our witness to Christ, or suffer in sharing
the sufferings of others, we are paying the price of being
human and being Christians in this world.

The Spirit of Christ promises the power to lift ordinary
human suffering into a participation in the sufferings of the
Savior. But it remains true that the portrait of the Spirit-
enabled person is painted on a canvas of pain.

The Bible does not provide psychological devices to get us
to take pleasure in our suffering. Christian suffering is not
sanctified neurosis. We still want desperately not to have to
experience our pain or our loss. The call of Christ is to
accept what we do not want, to accept it and discover enabling grace within it.

The apostle Paul quite naturally wanted to be rid of his
own thorn in the flesh. Instead he received grace sufficient
to bear it. But he was not relieved of his desire to be free of
it. Had he no desire to be rid of it, he would not have
suffered from it—and would have needed no grace to bear

it. His suffering was genuine and human. But grace enabled him to turn genuine human suffering into genuine Christian growth.

We do not mean to contend that God's will is the cause of all our suffering anymore than we wish anyone to believe that personal demons are the cause. But what we are saying is that whatever the cause of our suffering, we have no Christian grounds for assuming that God will assuredly rescue us from it by a miracle.

Suffering is a painful and unwanted condition of life on earth that, by the redemptive power of God's Spirit, can become the soil of sainthood or at least the catalyst for character.

And when we see our fellow Christians suffer, we are urged by the apostle Paul to share their burdens. We are not to encourage them to assume that all their burdens can be miraculously removed; we are told to bear their burdens with them (Gal. 6:2). This is the spiritual law for the Body of Christ: "if one member suffers, all suffer together" (1 Cor. 12:26). And, when we share in suffering, we can share in Christ's comfort, for, as Paul said, "we know that as you share in our sufferings, you will also share in our comfort" (2 Cor. 1:7). Again, the picture is this: expect to suffer with Christ, but be encouraged while you suffer, for the church suffers with you while you suffer with Christ.

True, in the perfect kingdom of God no one will have to suffer. "He will wipe away every tear . . . and death shall be no more, neither shall there be mourning nor crying nor pain any more, for the former things have passed away" (Rev. 21:4). The vision of the City of God matches the human longing to suffer no more. But we are not yet living in the New Jerusalem; the former things have not all passed away. We live and we suffer in hope—and hope of eventual freedom enables us to suffer now with grace.

We are speaking, of course, of pain and loss that we cannot relieve by our own decision or by medical treatment. Christ does not forbid us to take action against suffering.

Everything about the gospel of loving empathy motivates us to relieve suffering wherever we can. But he does warn us not to expect that our action will always be effective, certainly not permanently effective, but rather to expect that when we cannot avoid it, suffering may be God's invitation to growth in holiness and grace.

Absence of suffering is a good, but not the highest good that God wills for all of us all of the time. We do not have an inalienable right to relief from suffering anymore than we have entitlement to perpetual health. Rather, we have a caution that the Christian should expect to suffer in this life. And we have an assurance that the Spirit of God enables us to experience our suffering as a share of Christ's own suffering and therefore a share in his redemption of the world of suffering.

Suffering with Christ may be God's redemptive way of healing people who experience ills they passionately wish would go away. Acceptance of our own unrelieved suffering in faith that God is wholly good may be a superior form of health. And using his sufficient grace to turn suffering into redemptive living may be the greatest miracle of healing.

We are healed in many ways, just as we enjoy health on several levels of being. We are healed when diseased cells are purged and revitalized. We are healed when malignant growths are excised from our vital organs. We are healed when disabling neuroses or psychoses are overcome and we are able again to live peaceably and constructively. We are healed as we are released from demonic powers. And we are also healed when we have the courage and patience to accept what we cannot change, endure what we cannot escape, find joy in the midst of pain, and live in hope while we suffer for the time being.

All this has a profound bearing on seminary training. Since most people who suffer are not miraculously relieved, we do very well indeed if we can equip men and women for a ministry that enables suffering people to believe that God is not rejecting them, but is calling them to

endure their suffering with courage and hope while they
await their ultimate glory. We know from the gospel that
every member of the body of Christ is called to suffer with
Christ, and we know from experience that relatively few are
privileged with miraculous release from suffering. Therefore, we seem summoned to prepare those who suffer to
receive that triumphant form of healing available to all
God's hurting children—redemptive suffering. Faith in
God's perfect goodness amid the pains and losses we devoutly wish to go away—this, too, is healing quite wonderful, not spectacular to be sure, but real, and in the long run
as divine as any healing can be.

5

Credibility and the Miraculous

As we consider the place of the miraculous in the training of men and women for ministry, we must be concerned with credibility. It is possible that in our enthusiasm for miraculous healings or exorcisms we may cause needless confusion and even unnecessary offense. Therefore, the training of ministers must include a wholesome commitment to credible service especially in ministries heavily devoted to the miraculous.

Credibility in any Christian ministry of healing must be established at two levels, the level of fact and the level of interpretation. On the level of fact, we must be transparently ready to submit our claims of healing to the most rigorous of empirical testing. On the level of interpretation, we need to make clear to the Christian community and to the world that we are not catering to sub-Christian clamor for instant relief from individual suffering and that any temporary, even though miraculous, healing of individual ailments is a very minor theme in Christian ministry compared to the deeper needs of God's people and God's world.

Our concern for credibility is intensified by the fact that

miracles of healing are not a monopoly of Christian ministries. They occur in folk religions everywhere. And we maintain our Christian credibility only to the extent that we submit our claims to objective testing for validity, integrating them into a larger Christian context so that their Christian meaning is distinct.

"Miracles" are common in tribal religions where the shaman, master of ecstasy, performs spectacular feats amid hysteria and rapture. In folk Islam, folk Buddhism, and folk Hinduism, various specialists practice the miraculous; some are magicians, others are medicine men and witchdoctors, and still others deal in the manipulation of the spirits that haunt the air. All of them routinely report wonderful successes at healing through their magical ministrations. In high Islam we even find saints and sadhus who perform magic works of resurrection, along with fakirs and dervishes whose talent is limited to ecstatic healings. But here, too, reports of healings are commonplace.

Folk religion abounds today on the fringes of Western culture. New Age cults are claiming divinity for people. Spiritualist organizations are thriving. All of them cater to a popular sense that we not only are entitled to glowing well-being, but that there must be a secret key available for boundless and holistic health. The initiated have the key, and they are willing to share it with others, almost always at a price; we are said to be fools for not claiming it.

Many of the health cults offer the philosophical insights of Eastern gurus to lead us to the god within us. Others use esoteric jargon to cloak in mystery common psychological techniques that are available from any therapist. And still others promise the power of magic and divinity to bring wholeness and healing to any sincere seeker.

Two things are noteworthy about the claims of healing in folk religions and cults. The first is that their reports are numerous and plausible. The second is that they are done in a spiritual context utterly different from and hostile to the Christian gospel. We must be aware of both, lest Christian claims of miraculous healing be substantially indistinct from the magic and hysteria of the cults.

A. Credibility of Claims

We must, in training ministers, missionaries, and psychologists who may engage in the ministry of miraculous healings, stress the importance of modesty and reserve in the face of understandable temptation to herald too soon the wonders of healing. Christian ministers ought to be ready always to subject any report of miraculous healing to objective, rigorous, and scientifically responsible testing. The tests should extend over an adequate period of time and be open to the critical examination of skeptics. Making claims without the controls of careful testing reduces objective credibility—especially in the eyes of the skeptics—to the level of the shaman, the magician, and the manipulator of voodoo. The credibility of Christian ministry should be many notches higher.

In this vein, Christian ministers must remember that ministerial credibility is not measured by the sincerity of the credulous. The fact that many people put credence in reports of miracles does not make the reports credible. Because people believe does not mean that what they believe merits belief. Credulity rises from deep desire that something be true. Credibility is earned by reliable and trustworthy testing.

B. Credibility of Christian Interpretation of the Miracles Reported

In training men and women who may engage in miraculous healing, we must educate them well to understand the difference between the report of a miracle and the interpretation of whatever it was that happened.

There is a difference between someone's glad report that he or she was miraculously healed and an understanding that God was at work redemptively in what happened. If we do not keep the difference in focus, we may reduce the miraculous to the same level of value as the magic of the shaman.

The difference between God and a shaman is not that God does better magic. The difference between Christianity and folk religions is not that Christianity has stronger medicine. The Lord Christ is not a magician.

One mark of the difference between Christian hope and magic healing is that, particularly since the death, resurrection, and ascension of Christ, evil spirits are not sovereignly autonomous, free to roam the air and occupy the bodies and souls of anyone they take a notion to assault with slings and arrows of disease and death. The evil spirits are not lords over life; Lordship belongs to Christ.

Another difference is that Christian faith caters neither to the narcissistic assumption that health is the highest of all goods nor to a gratuitous assumption that God exists to deliver on demand the health and welfare we may claim as our inalienable right.

The gospel does not clearly vindicate itself to the world when ministers proclaim the occasional release of affluent individuals from bearable aches and pains while thousands of starving children call in vain to be fed and thousands of oppressed people plead in vain for justice. Signs and wonders cannot point credibly to the redemptive power of Christ unless they happen in a living context of concern and passion for peace and justice. Without authentic passion for those fundamental social realities of the kingdom of God, evangelical ministries famous for performing miraculous healings will lack credibility among discerning men and women.

It is of utmost importance to understand that though the power of Christ is sometimes demonstrated in victorious public confrontation with Satan, the gospel is more than a disclosure of magic that matches and outdoes the magic of folk religions and cults. Its agenda includes much more than instant relief from the pains of life. The gospel is the good news of Christ's victory over sin and all its dark effects on human life. It is a summons to wait and to struggle in hope for the coming of God's kingdom of peace and justice, as well as of the perfect and permanent healing of individuals.

In the light of the importance of credibility in Christian ministry, we who minister by training men and women to minister must make credibility a high priority in our educational enterprise. It is not our task to discourage anyone from ministering to the sick and afflicted with prayers for miraculous healing. It is our responsibility to encourage them to establish Christian credibility, lest in their enthusiasm for the miraculous they actually discredit the ministry. We must then nurture a sober modesty and couple this with a passionate reluctance to make claims for miracles without a corresponding readiness to submit them both to objective testing and to theological interpretation.

6

The Distinctives
of Fuller Theological
Seminary

We move now from our general observations about miraculous healing to the character of Fuller Theological Seminary as it relates to the place of miraculous healing within our curriculum.

Fuller has a sacred calling to be in fact and in deed what it publicly declares itself to be. It also bears responsibility to help others to perceive us in ways true to what we are and intend to be. Fuller has an evangelically defined character that we aim to express theologically, pastorally, and academically. As the faculty, we share accountability both for Fuller's actual faithfulness to that character and for preventing distortion of it in public perception.

We have together affirmed our purpose to be "an evangelical, multidenominational, international, and multiethnic community dedicated to the preparation of men and women for the manifold ministries of Christ and his Church . . . through graduate education, professional development, and spiritual formation." We shape and test our curriculum in the light of this purpose. And in its light we make the following observations.

A. Fuller's Evangelical Commitment

The theological heart of Fuller Seminary is unyielding in
its commitment to evangelical faith and practice. The evangelical theology at the core of our academic existence is
derived from the historic Christian tradition, especially as it
was reformed and renewed in the Protestant Reformation
and again as that great work of God on the Continent was in
turn enriched through the faith and piety of Wesleyan and
other evangelistic movements in Great Britain and the
United States. Our evangelical commitment disposes us
strongly to the theology of the Reformation; but we are neither cultic evangelical nor sectarian Reformed. We embrace
within our faculty men and women who represent, among
others, the Pentecostal, the Anabaptist, and the Anglican
traditions, and we treasure the many incalculable ways they
have enriched and sometimes corrected our classic evangelical ethos. Further, we accept with thanks to our one Lord,
the opportunities we have to serve many communions, the
currents of whose histories run alongside of rather than
within the evangelical mainstream.

Our commitment to be a seminary that is thoroughly
evangelical, neither cultic nor sectarian but truly multidenominational, permits us freely to follow the Spirit of
Christ into new understandings of Christian truth and new
ventures in Christian ministry. Our commitment is not
a foreclosure on change and reform; indeed, it compels
us, under the guidance of Holy Scripture, to seek and encourage innovative strategies and pioneering programs
that will enable the Church of Christ to perform ever more
effectively its many ministries among the peoples of the
world.

Our evangelical commitment does not define in advance
the parameters of change. We know that we are vulnerable to
curricular innovation and classroom strategies that could
subtly subvert our theological basis and, rather than enrich
our evangelical tradition, deflect us from it. Yet we must

take the risk. And we must also, for this reason, constantly evaluate significant shifts of emphases or direction.

Thus, it is in faithfulness to our evangelical character and identity that we reflect on both the theological implications and the academic propriety of including scheduled sessions of prayer for miraculous healing within seminary courses, especially when such sessions illustrate and support a view of ministry that may be uncongenial to the evangelical tradition.

Historically, miraculous healing has not had a leading, certainly not a central place in evangelical ministries. Evangelicals have given priority to the preaching of the Word of God, to the sacraments, and to diaconal ministries of relief for the sick and the poor of our world. Evangelical ministries have, of course, included public prayers of faith for the healing of sick people. But the expectation has been that God would normally answer prayers for healing through the medical means he has providentially given to us. To be sure, prayers for miraculous healings that exceed or even confound ordinary medical expectations, are on the evangelical agenda, and such prayers are sometimes answered. But traditional evangelical ministries have not specialized in public services of healing in which worshippers are encouraged to expect that their sicknesses will be cured then and there, directly and without medical mediation, by an act of the Spirit.

Nor have evangelical ministries encouraged the belief that miraculous healing is a special sign of genuine faith and effective prayer. Far more likely, the renewal of godliness in personal life and revival of righteousness in public life have been the signs looked for to attest the work of the Spirit in our ministries.

In the light of the sort of evangelical institution we are, then, the faculty is obliged to monitor courses that conduct sessions of healing and exorcism as a regular and climactic feature. We need to monitor the academic propriety of them, of course, but also their theological premises. Our responsibility increases to the extent that the method and emphasis in ministry promoted in a given course are not in accord with traditional evangelical theologies of ministry. And, needless to say, our concern is compounded when those who teach such courses are not full-time members of the Fuller faculty, accountable to their colleagues for the content and tenor of their teaching.

We have no desire to disparage or to discount the ministry of any person or group outside of Fuller Theological Seminary. What we intend is to be true to ourselves, our tradition, and our character as an evangelical seminary meeting the challenges of evangelical ministry today.

B. Fuller's Multidenominational Ministry

Fuller is dedicated to the ministries of dozens of denominations. We are committed to the training of ministers for a lifetime of loyal service within their respective churches. Being multidenominational involves far more than our privilege of having the riches of a beautifully diverse student community. It means that we have a profound trust to honor, a trust that leaders and members of denominations place in us to support and not to subvert students in their loyalty to the communions in whose ministries they will serve.

When any course at Fuller tends to make students highly critical of their denomination's traditional forms of ministry, we must be sensitive to how that course affects our multidenominational trust. Many of the major denominations do not include miraculous healing in their normal ministries. Indeed, the theological emphases and ministerial styles characteristic of many ministries of the miraculous are uncongenial to some of the major denominations that Fuller serves. We cannot, therefore, be uncritical of any course where practices are carried on and publicized that are incompatible with the faith and practices of the churches in whose ministry most of our students intend to serve.

As a multidenominational seminary we have a peculiar
trust to keep. We are known to offer students an educational
experience that includes great diversity. And we respect the
freedom of those students who change their church alliances
while with us. Yet we make an implicit commitment to the
denominations not to allow our diversity to be an occasion
for undermining denominational loyalty.

C. *Fuller's Faculty Consensus*

Fuller Seminary's commitment to both an evangelical
theology and to a multidenominational ministry requires an
ongoing respect for the faculty consensus that has developed
out of our shared commitment to the stated purposes of the
seminary. Our consensus is of our essence. We are not super-
intended by an ecclesiastical monitor; we need to be our
own monitors, and we need constantly to attend to our consensus. And though we are a faculty of many nuances in
points of view, traditions, spiritualities, and styles, we have
been remarkably blessed with a continuous consensus in
faith and practice.

Our consensus is delicately flexible, yet definite and limit-
ing. It is focused theologically by our explicitly evangelical
statement of faith. Yet it is accommodating in ministerial
styles and emphases. All the more reason then to guard it
and keep it with all diligence.

So much about the life of Fuller depends on faculty consensus that whenever any new trend or startling innovation
threatens it, we need to assess the trend, not only as to its
intrinsic merits, but as to its effect on our consensus. This is
peculiarly true with respect to curriculum and with all that
goes on in the formal education at Fuller. Our consensus is
more important to us than is any single course. Division in
the faculty is more serious than the loss of any single curricular offering or the sidetracking of anyone's private agenda.

Consensus is not threatened whenever some faculty members disagree with what other faculty members teach about

controversial issues. For instance, consensus is not necessarily threatened when a faculty member holds a minority conviction about the validity of "signs and wonders" in the contemporary church. Nor is it threatened whenever some faculty members disapprove of how other faculty members conduct their classes. For instance, it is not threatened by the fact that some teachers depend wholly on lectures while others make extensive use of case studies.

But consensus would be threatened if a featured classroom practice became a *cause célèbre,* and bid well to become a public signal that Fuller has altered its course or changed its character. The consensus would also be threatened if an opinion were encouraged that what happens in a unique classroom event is the state of spiritual art and the authentically biblical form of Christian ministry for our time—and that the majority of the faculty, who do not share enthusiasm for it, represent a powerless evangelical intellectualism.

Consensus, the vital link between Fuller's past and future, is our common sense of what we are, what we believe, and what we can do together. It is our way of keeping our identity amid constant and necessary change. So important is it, that we dare not challenge it too far.

D. Fuller as an Academic Institution

As an academic community dedicated to Christian ministry, Fuller serves the churches without being a church. It is, on the other hand, also a Christian community and its members engage regularly in common worship; prayer and praise are at the center of the community's life. Yet, the liturgical life at the core of the academic life does not turn a school into a church, nor make it less of an academic community.

As scholars in a graduate academic institution, Fuller faculty are expected to investigate with all scholarly receptiveness and rigor any phenomena related to their disciplines.

With respect to healing, we particularly encourage those scholars who explore the frontiers of ministry; we think especially of our missiologists and psychologists.

We encourage our scholars to search relentlessly and freely into all the dynamic relationships between spirit and body, faith and health, prayer and healing. We encourage them to investigate the influence of the demonic in human life, in its physical as well as its moral and psychic dimensions, and to study and test all appropriate methods for releasing people from demonic power. And we encourage the appropriate scholars of our three schools to develop an integrative program for the ongoing study of spiritual healing.

Our problem at Fuller is not a reluctance to encourage inquiry into all possibilities of healing. It is rather a question of how we can pursue the inquiry in an academically and theologically responsible manner. In this context, our question concerns itself also with the sorts of practice appropriate to the academic classrooms.

As an academic community serving the churches, a theological seminary must do some things that simulate a church service without being a church service. So, some things are appropriate to both a classroom and a sanctuary. But other things appropriate to one are not at all appropriate to another. And some things may be on the borderline; we do not have an infallible sense of what is appropriate in a Fuller classroom. Thus we need to practice considerable tolerance.

Yet at the same time there are useful criteria which need to be taken into consideration. One criterion is *academic accountability:* whatever is done in a laboratory situation should be subject to evaluation and criticism within that classroom. Indeed, the classroom teacher is obligated to encourage the development of acceptable standards for evaluating what is going on in his or her classroom. This is what happens, for instance, in a preaching class or a clinic.

In any session of miraculous healing, a person's experience of a miracle may tend to become the criterion for the reality of a miracle. What a person reports of his or her experience could be taken to establish the claim that a miracle has indeed happened. And to open the process to on-the-spot evaluation can seem out of keeping with the tone of the service. Critical evaluation of the process is likely to be felt as an unbelieving intrusion into the ministry of the Spirit. In short, sessions of prayer for miraculous healing have tended to resist the sort of readiness for criticism that an academic setting requires.

For this reason, any course in which miraculous healing sessions are a scheduled and prominent feature should be monitored carefully.

Another criterion is *pastoral accountability.* Where the pastoral ministry of healing is practiced, appropriate pastoral responsibility must be assumed. The fact is that in healing services, some people who want to be healed are not healed. And the fact is that some people who believe they were permanently healed suffer relapses into the same illness from which they believed themselves cured. We must take great care not to create severe personal crises without the provision of pastoral care for the disillusioned and confused. The classroom offers limited opportunity for pastoral care to the disappointed. The church offers more possibility for ongoing pastoral care.

If it is important for students to have firsthand experience with public services of healing, the most appropriate place for them to have it is within the congregation where it can be practiced with pastoral accountability, and where students can benefit through field work study under academic supervision. Prayer for healing, however, may be appropriate in certain classroom settings.

Still another criterion is that of *faculty accountability.* A faculty is accountable for what happens in the courses it approves for academic credit. It should be able to support or defend any course that it approves for academic credit. And what is true of the faculty as a whole, is acutely true of the professor of record. No assigned teacher of any course, especially of a course that has become a public event, may

surrender his or her accountability to a guest, particularly
when the guest teacher also carries on a widely publicized
and critically debated form of ministry within the classroom.

In view of what we have said about faculty accountability,
we must raise a doubt as to whether we can accept accountability for a course that by virtue of its goals and methods is
not open to normal academic critique.

In this section, we have been holding up the theological
and academic character of Fuller as a measure by which to
evaluate both the propriety of conducting sessions of miraculous healing as a prominent and regular feature of a Fuller
course, and the theological and academic integrity of the
course itself. Therefore, in the light of what Fuller is, we urge
the faculty to consider critically both the theological pre-
suppositions behind and the academic credentials of any
such course. We have no right, let alone obligation, to approve or to disapprove of courses simply because they are
popular and widely spoken of. But we do have an obligation
to foster critical, yet believing investigation into the possibilities of healing ministries. Thus, we believe the faculty
should endorse and support critical exploration into all the
dimensions of miraculous healing and exorcism so that,
with scholarly methods and scriptural criteria, we may
more responsibly serve the churches as they seek out authentically biblical ministries of healing for the suffering people
of our world.

7

Miraculous Healing
and Responsible Ministry

The Fuller faculty is as dedicated to a ministry that demonstrates the power of God in human life as it is in conveying the truth of the gospel. We hate barren intellectualism; we have no truck with the arid notion that being a disciple of Christ implies no more than having right opinions about him. We want men and women to enter the ministry with the expectation that the Lord will be present with them in power. Whatever their individual gifts and strengths, and in whatever type of ministry they serve, whether in preaching, counseling, alleviating poverty, social reform, or miraculous healings, we pray that all of their ministries will be a demonstration of the "immeasurable greatness of his power . . ." (Eph. 1:19).

We have a magnificent obligation to students. Our respect for the healing presence of God should certainly be transparent to our students. Nothing we say or do should discourage them from anticipating that their ministries can truly be, by God's grace, empowered by the Spirit.

Precisely because we owe them respect for spiritual power, we owe them something besides. We owe them training for responsibility in the exercise of whatever power God allows them to have in ministry; and training also in the protection of God's people from charlatans and abusers of spiritual power.

With an eye to responsibility in ministry, particularly in healing ministries, the Fuller faculty owes its students direction and encouragement in several areas. We shall focus on a few areas of special concern.

A. *The Discernment of Spirits*

Discernment is the indispensable gift we all need to recognize and approve what is excellent in life (Phil. 1:9) and thus to lead lives "worthy of the Lord" (Col. 1:10). Thus, discernment is a gift God wills for all of us.

It also appears that God gives to some of his children the special power to discern between the presence of his Spirit and the presence of alien spirits (1 Cor. 12:10). Presumably, the gift is also extended to distinguish between the influence of evil spirits and natural phenomena. We have reason to be grateful for anyone within the Christian community who has been given this gift.

But as is true of our exercise of any of God's gifts, this gift, perhaps above all others, must be exercised with great care and reserve, especially when it is used to discern the presence of evil spirits in people.

When any group concedes to anyone the power to see what others cannot see, to sense what others cannot sense and to know what others cannot know, it also concedes unusual power to that gifted person. And when the group not only acknowledges the gift to discern the presence of evil spirits, but the power as well of exorcising them, it concedes dangerous power. All power is vulnerable to misuse, but never more than when it is spiritual power exercised over people whom someone discerns to have an evil spirit.

Discernment of spirits can become the tyranny of the

discerning. Therefore, within any Christian community this power must be conceded only with critical discretion and used only with humble submission to the community's open critique.

No moment is more critical to a compassionate ministry than the moment when someone claims to discern the presence of demons in another person's life. The risk is compounded when someone claims to know that demons have taken full possession of a person, and that exorcism is the appropriate remedy.

The danger is perhaps greatest when a child is involved. The potential for harm in a child's life after a "discerner" mistakenly intuits that he or she is possessed by a demon is very real. Sacred human rights could be violated by irresponsible discerners. Who is to protect children against such abuse? Certainly the Christian community bears a special responsibility for protecting the little ones in its care against those who abuse the gift of discernment.

An evangelical ministry must above all resist any temptation to surrender its critical faculties to people who claim to have discernment.

Anyone may claim the gift. But how is the claim recognized and validated? What are the discerner's credentials? What are the signals that give demons away to the discerning? How do we know when behavior is so evil or so irrational that it surely signals possession by demons? How do we perceive who really knows in any specific instance? Who has the gift to discern the true discerners? And who controls the exorcisers?

Our faculty owes to students whatever help it can give in developing standards for testing the discernment of discerners, especially those who claim to be able to discern the presence of evil spirits in persons, and in developing standards as well for the practice of exorcism. What sorts of standards might they be? Perhaps we could make a few suggestions:

1. Discernment, unlike divine revelation, is the ability to detect the real differences between things that are otherwise not open to the view of everyone else. Since discernment does not confer infallibility it is therefore open to judgment and confirmation by disinterested critics who have their own views of the same phenomena. All discernment of the demonic in people, therefore, should be subject to the evaluation of wise, informed, and responsible members of the Christian community.

2. No one should ever be subject to exorcism without informed consent.

3. Only persons recognized by their communities to be spiritually mature, responsible, and wise Christians should ever be permitted to exorcise demons from anyone.

4. Wherever it is possible to do so, the Christian community should seek the counsel and the active involvement of professional people trained to evaluate bizarre and destructive behavior; it should approve of no exorcism unless the person to be exorcised has been evaluated and treated by people trained and skilled in diagnosis and therapy.

5. Exorcisms should not be done in secret nor kept secret. For the protection of the persons involved, as well as for later study, appropriate records should be kept of both the diagnosis and the actual exorcism. All such records should, of course, be subject to informed consent and should be kept in confidence. But where consent is given, they should be made available to both students and critics.

While we are sensitive to life's mysterious vulnerability to destructive demonic forces, we are highly sensitive to the need for a high level of responsibility in any actual diagnosis of demons as the cause of physical disease, mental illness or moral turpitude. The need for controls is intensified a thousandfold when those who discern the demonic also claim the power to exorcise. It may be as important to protect people from exorcists as to protect them from demons.

B. Keeping Priorities Clear

For thousands of people who survive on the fringes of starvation, and for those who care for them, occasional healing of a few physical ailments may not appear as an overpowering demonstration of God's power to save the world. For people engaged in struggles against the hunger and oppression suffered by many multitudes, occasional miraculous healings, especially of relatively minor ailments, may not seem like "signs and wonders" of God's power and presence in the world. When such miracles are celebrated out of proportion to their real significance, they may seem to be signs, not of God's reality in our world, but of our trivialized expectations.

We recognize this fact: to those who have anguished compassion for the massive suffering of the people of our broken and oppressive world, it is offensive to be told that God uniquely proves himself as Savior by the occasional healing of diseases which may be borne with grace or might be healed by ordinary means. The gospel itself causes necessary offense to the proud; we must not cause needless offense to the weak.

The priorities of the gospel call for the proclamation of forgiveness and for seeking justice, doing mercy, and walking humbly through life in stride with the victorious and compassionate Savior. Perhaps it was with such priorities in mind that both Jesus and Paul depreciated popular craving for signs. And it must have been at least partly out of the same true sense of priority that the great Reformers, Calvin and Luther, and the great evangelists, Whitefield, Finney, Moody, Fuller, and Graham, among others, were blessed with ministries of life-changing and epoch-transforming spiritual power but who yet never encouraged miraculous healing as a public feature of their historic undertakings for God.

The faculty of Fuller can, in this age when Christian

people seek after spectacular signs, help prepare students to keep their priorities straight whenever they enter or are encouraged to engage in a miraculous ministry of healing.

C. *Honesty in Ministry*

Looking forward to the sorts of persons the church would need when the long, hellish war was finished, Dietrich Bonhoeffer said that our need would be first of all for honest, straightforward persons—not geniuses or brilliant tacticians, but simple, honest people. There is certainly need for integrity in the Christian churches, especially where the miraculous is the focus of attention and where expectations of the spectacular are encouraged. Precisely where much is promised and much is claimed, temptations to be less than honest are greatest.

To the extent that we are eager to sustain people's interests, hopes, and expectations, we are tempted to exaggerate successes and disguise failures. We who teach at Fuller have an obligation to exemplify and to urge honesty before students as a quality more important to God than their success, and certainly more important than their fame. Honesty in a crooked world is not as spectacular as healing in a hurting world, but in the long run it is a stronger sign of God's power.

One requirement of honesty in a public ministry of healing is full and accurate reporting, both to the faithful and to the world-at-large. The minister who engages in healing should publicize his or her failures as loudly as the successes. Chronicles of healings should include failed attempts to heal, prayers for healing that were answered in death, apparent healings of people who soon relapsed into the disease from which they were healed—all of this alongside of the grateful reports of success. Reports that ignore these and tell only of the successes are, we insist, disingenuous exercises in pious deception.

In urging honesty in the ministry of healing we are asking for no more than we expect of the ministry of evangelism.

No work of God is served when ministers give misleading reports of conversions to Christ, where failures and disappointments are covered up or disguised. Thus when we urge honesty in the ministry of healing we are asking for nothing but the simple integrity the Lord demands of all his servants.

Another requirement of honesty in healing is an open subjection of one's claims to rigorous, long-term, and objective testing. Honesty, and the public appearance of honesty, may require that healing ministries defer so much as public thanks for specific healings until they have been exposed to careful examination over a period of time. And more immediately, it requires us to permit any interested reporter to investigate every aspect of a healing ministry.

Being honest with a person suffering from a serious, life-threatening illness is especially urgent. It is particularly needed when the ill person is disposed to defer medical treatment in the expectations of a miracle. Such people must be urged to subject themselves to professional medical care even while other persons pray for a miracle.

One more demand of honesty lies not with claims of healing but with the diagnosis of disease. Honest ministers engaged in healing will make it clear they are not diagnosticians and do not accept at face value the diagnosis that people report to them when they come for healing. And honest ministers of healing will explain to people that what sometimes feels like a divine miracle could be God working through a not uncommon psychological experience.

Against the lure of benevolent fakery and altruistic abridgment of truth, the Fuller faculty must promote integrity as one thing without which both they and their students should never venture into any ministry.

D. *Miraculous Healing in a Culture of Entitlements*

Students of our culture tell us that most modern Americans believe they have an inalienable right to personal fulfillment and happiness. Entitlement to a pain-free, disappointment-free, and frustration-free life, they tell us, has become a basic tenet of our time. Not duty but rights, not commitment but self-maximization, not the possibility of patient suffering but the guarantee of instant entitlement—these are the creeds of what Robert Bellah calls our "therapeutic culture."

We cannot avoid the question whether the current Christian expectation of miraculous healing manifests the same syndrome. We cannot avoid it, if only because others, unsympathetic to the gospel, are asking it. Fuller faculty are obliged at least to engage students with the question: do some aspects of the current healing movement encourage and perhaps express the cultural creed of personal entitlements?

We have spoken earlier of a paradigm-shift. But our paradigms of reality include our attitudes and values, and our sense of what is coming to us, as much as they include the way we view the possibility that evil spirits can influence or control our lives. The burgeoning ministries of miraculous healing could signal a paradigm-shift away from the biblical world in which all of us are called to be servants and in which none of us has inherent rights to earthly health and happiness. We would encourage Christians everywhere to test their spirits to be sure that their expectation of healing is not inspired by a false worldly claim of entitlement to freedom from all pain or by a worldly belief that perpetual enjoyment of physical health is the most important of human values.

We have in this section underscored our pastoral concern that any ministry of miraculous healing be carried on with shared accountability. Pastors should be keenly sensitive to the special temptations that beset anyone who has or believes he or she has the gift of healing. And we, as a faculty, accept our responsibility for bringing these temptations to the consciousness of our students.

We caution against misuse and abuse of God's remarkable gifts but in no way reject them or discourage their use in the churches. Indeed, when we warn against the exaggeration of this particular gift's importance and against abuse of that power, we mean at the same time to express our gratitude to God for this precious, if precarious ministry.

Epilogue

As we bring our report to a close, we affirm again our faith in the power of God to renew and restore life in every part. All that we have written here is rooted in and shaped by our gratitude for "the immeasurable greatness of his power in us who believe" (Eph. 1:19). We are committed to the service of Christ whose living Spirit is able to restore wholeness to the human spirit and health to the human body. And we are committed equally to the ministry of Christ who, as Lord of all, will bring peace to the nations and justice to the people of the world.

We affirm our faith in the power, as well as the truth of the gospel; we are committed to the truth biblically informed, systematically stated, and cogently defended. We distance ourselves from any intellectualism that could shrink the gospel of Christ to arid formulae, just as we reject the abuses of power cut adrift from truth.

As we have prepared this report we have together been led to a renewed awareness that Christ is the Healer of the whole person and the whole of life, just as we have been led together to appeal for care and responsibility in the exercise of his healing gifts. So we offer this report with praise to the Lord of saving truth and healing power and we offer it with thanks to God that he permits us, earthen vessels, to minister to needy people in confidence that our ministry is infused with the enabling power of his Spirit and informed with the truth of the gospel.